WOMEN
IN HISTORY

WOMEN
AND WAR

A. Susan Williams

Wayland

WOMEN
IN HISTORY

Women and the Arts
Women and Business
Women and Education
Women and the Family
Women and Literature
Women and Politics
Women and Science
Women and Sport
Women and War
Women and Work

Series editor: Catherine Ellis
Consultant: Professor Deirdre Beddoe BA, PhD, Dip Ed, Reader in History at The Polytechnic of Wales
Designer: Joyce Chester

Front cover: Painting by Edward F. Skinner, *For King and Country*.
Back cover: Top left – Florence Nightingale (1820–1910). Top right – members of the Women's Land Army during the First World War. Bottom left – Pauline Cutting (b. 1952) in Beirut camp. Bottom right – First World War munitions workers.

First published in 1989 by
Wayland (Publishers) Limited
61 Western Road, Hove
East Sussex BN3 1JD, England

© Copyright 1989 Wayland (Publishers) Limited

British Library Cataloguing in Publication Data
Williams, A. Susan
    Women and war. – Women in history
    1. Wars. Role of women, 1900–
    I. Title   II. Series
    909.82

    ISBN 1–85210–503–8

Typeset by Kalligraphics Limited, Horley, Surrey
Printed in Italy by G. Canale & C.S.p.A., Turin
Bound in the UK by Mac Lehose & Partners, Portsmouth

Picture acknowledgements
The pictures in this book were supplied by the following: Camera Press 15 (top), 17, 37 (bottom) (Colman Doyle), 38 (G/M), 40 (Times), 43 (Homer Sykes); Hulton Picture Library back cover top left, 9 (bottom), 19, 20, 21, 41 (both), 42; Trustees of the Imperial War Museum front cover (Edward F. Skinner 'For King and Country'), 8 (top), 12, 13, 14, 16, 29 (bottom), 36; Mary Evans Picture Library 5 (both), 6, 7, 11 (both), 22 (Fawcett Library), 34–5; Marx Memorial Library 23 (both), 24 (top), 25; Peter Newark's Historical Pictures 4, 31, 32 (top); Peter Newark's Military Pictures 29 (top); Topham back cover bottom left, back cover top right, 9 (top), 10, 15 (bottom) 18, 24 (bottom), 26, 27, 28, 30, 32 (bottom), 33, 37 (top), 39; Wayland Picture Library back cover bottom right, 8 (bottom).

Permissions
The publishers would like to thank the following for permitting the use of certain extracts in the quotations: Jonathan Cape Ltd; Oxford University Press; Pandora Press; Pluto Publishing Ltd; George Sassoon for 'Glory of Women' by Siegfried Sassoon; Virago Press; the extracts from *Testament of Youth* by Vera Brittain are included with the permission of her literary executors and Victor Gollancz Ltd.

Contents

Boadicea leading her people in revolt against the Roman Army in AD 60. She was eventually defeated but displayed tremendous courage.

Introduction

When many of us think of war, the first image that springs to mind is that of men engaged in combat. If we think of women at all, it is of them mourning the death of their men. Such images have a sound basis in British history before the nineteenth century, for usually it *was* men who took on the role of fighter. Traditionally women stayed at home, taking care of the children and keeping 'the home fires burning'. Female warriors like Boadicea, who led her people into battle against the Roman Army in AD 60, were remarkable because they were exceptional.

In the last two centuries, however, British women have been increasingly drawn into war. In the First and Second World Wars, women produced the munitions for the battlefield and also went to the Front. Today, they are valuable members of military medical units and of the armed forces. However, the major element of women's involvement in war is their role as civilians. Modern warfare makes little distinction between those who stay at home and those who fight. Weapons and communications have become so sophisticated that everybody is now a potential target for attack. In the first half of the Second World War, more British women and children were killed at home in Britain by bombing raids than their fighting men. When the first atomic bombs were dropped on the Japanese cities of Hiroshima and Nagasaki in 1945, almost everybody – men, women and children – was killed.

This book gives an account of the various ways in which British women have been involved in war from the turn of the nineteenth century to the late twentieth century. It also traces the development of the women's peace movement from the outbreak of the First World War. We shall see women coping with the violence of war as fighters, as workers, as victims, as mothers and as pacifists.

1

Women and War

1800–1902

During the Napoleonic Wars at the beginning of the nineteenth century, in which Britain fought against France, the British Army and Navy were much, much smaller than the armed forces we have today. As a result, fewer families were directly affected by the fighting. It is not surprising, then, that the war plays only a minor role in the fiction of Jane Austen, who lived through it. She died just two years after the Battle of Waterloo in 1815, when the British and the Prussians finally defeated Napoleon. In *Pride and Prejudice,* as in all her novels, there are only brief references to the war – to a militia regiment and to the folly of girls who talk about 'nothing but officers'. The only consequence of the 'restoration of peace' is a change of home!

Between 1854 and 1856, Britain, France and Turkey were at war with Russia in the Crimean peninsula. Wounded British soldiers were taken care of by Florence Nightingale and her nurses at a hospital in Scutari. The Crimean War is often thought of as the first occasion when British women played any kind of a military role.

In fact, women had been nursing soldiers in battle zones long before this. These women were called 'camp followers', because they followed the troops. Today, the term is used to describe

Above *This woman and her children are camp followers travelling with the British Army during the Napoleonic Wars. The wives of soldiers and sailors used to follow their husbands on military expeditions, to cook and wash for them, and nurse them if they were wounded.*

6

[There was the] necessity of having [women] with an army to attend upon and help the sick and wounded, which men are unfit for. Had more women gone, I suppose that many had not perished as they did.
General Robert Venables, on the West Indies Campaign of 1656.

9

Left *Florence Nightingale and her nurses caring for the casualties of the Crimean War. Their hard work caused the hospital death-rate to fall dramatically.*

Below *Olive Schreiner, the South African writer who was placed under house arrest by the British Army during the Boer War. She believed there would be no more wars once women had 'an equal share in the control and governance of modern national life'.*

> ❛ ▬▬▬▬▬▬▬▬▬
> **No tinsel of trumpets and flags will ultimately seduce women into the insanity of recklessly destroying life, or gild the wilful taking of life with any other name than that of murder, whether it be the slaughter of the million or of one by one.** Olive Schreiner, *Woman and War,* 1911.
> ▬▬▬▬▬▬▬▬▬ ❜

prostitutes, but the camp followers of yesterday were usually the wives of the soldiers and sailors. During the Napoleonic Wars, sailors' wives were on board ship during battle and tended the wounded. Most camp followers were kept busy by their men, but some had a more varied existence. *The Life and Adventures of Mrs Christian Davis,* a book written by Daniel Defoe in 1740, is about a camp follower who at different times is a military housekeeper, a nurse, a laundress, a cook, a prostitute . . . *and* a soldier!

Camp followers came from the lower social classes and relied on army rations to survive. Perhaps this is why their contribution to the armed forces did not get much recognition. Florence Nightingale and her nurses, on the other hand, were from the middle and upper classes. They were therefore seen as 'proper' nurses with a good moral influence.

During the Anglo-Boer War (1899–1902), the British fought to take control of the Boer Republics in South Africa. Many British intellectuals protested against their nation's treatment of the Boers, and a few women went to see for themselves what was going on. Emily Hobhouse investigated conditions in the camps for prisoners, and published a scathing report about the behaviour of the British Army.

Another woman who entered the war zone was Lady Sarah Wilson, who was the correspondent in Mafeking for the *Daily Mail.* She succeeded in getting her stories to Britain and even managed to get a letter from Cecil Rhodes while he was besieged in the city of Kimberley. She was described as 'the good genius of the siege' and was said to have 'splendid pluck'; but this praise possibly had more to do with her support for the British side than for her work!

Few people in Britain were much bothered about the native South Africans, who were badly treated by both sides. Many were killed or forced off their land. One person who did care was the novelist Olive Schreiner, who was committed to the struggle for an independent South Africa in which all races would have equal rights. Schreiner was critical of the war, and especially of the British Army, which reacted by ransacking her house and burning the manuscript of a new book. She was placed under house arrest for six months, during which time she wrote down what she could remember of the book, with a British soldier on guard outside.

In 1911, Olive Schreiner sketched a link between women, motherhood and peace in *Woman and War.* Three years later, when the First World War broke out, this link became the foundation of many women's opposition to the war.

Florence Nightingale (1820–1910)

Florence Nightingale, the founder of modern nursing, was born into the upper classes and was expected to become a lady of leisure. She was appalled by this prospect and decided to become a nurse. Her family opposed the idea, because nursing at this time was a lower-class occupation and, in any case, hospitals were dirty and seedy places. Nightingale was determined, however. She studied medicine from books and went to train for a while in Germany.

She returned to London to become the superintendent of an Institution for the Care of Sick Gentlewomen in Distressed Circumstances. The secretary of state for war was so impressed by her efficiency that in 1854 he asked her to take a band of nurses to the Crimea, where Britain was at war with Russia. Large numbers of British soldiers were dying like flies in the Crimea because there was no proper medical treatment.

Nightingale and her nurses moved into the hospital barracks at Scutari just before the Battle of Inkerman. She organized supplies, arranged for mattresses to be made from straw, supervised the nurses, and provided warm food and drink. She became known as 'The Lady with the Lamp', because she toured the wards with her lamp last thing at night to bring comfort to the injured and the dying.

Nightingale came home in 1856 because of a serious illness, but did not stop working. She was anxious to reform the hospital administration of the British Army. Her *Notes on Matters Affecting the Health, Efficiency and Hospital Administration of the British Army* begins with the observation that, 'It may

Florence Nightingale laid the foundations of the nursing profession as we know it today.

seem a strange principle to enunciate as the very first requirement in a Hospital that it should do the sick no harm'!

Nightingale was now on the verge of collapse and had to work from her sick-bed. In 1860, she set up a school of nursing at St Thomas's Hospital in London and managed to supervise the nurses' training. Because of her influence, nursing began to be seen as a decent and useful profession for women of all classes. Within twenty years, there were trained nurses in most hospitals and a growing number of nursing schools. Nightingale went blind in 1901, nine years before her death. In 1907, she became the first woman to receive the Order of Merit.

Above and Below Typical recruitment posters from the First World War. They show women supporting their men's departure for the Front, and suggest that men ought to go to war to protect their women and children.

2

The First World War

1914–1918

The First World War was sparked off when the heir to the Austro–Hungarian throne was assassinated by Serbian nationalists while visiting Serbia. However, the real origins of the First World War lay more in the rivalry between European countries to expand and to protect their empires.

It was called a world war because twenty-eight countries from all over the globe took part, although some did little fighting. On one side there was Germany, the Austro-Hungarian Empire, Bulgaria and Turkey. On the other side there were the Allies – Britain, the Russian Empire, France, Belgium, Italy, Japan and some smaller countries. The USA joined the Allies in 1917, and its extra power helped to bring them victory.

Much of the war was fought in the trenches, which were cut deep in the ground of the battlefield by both sides. The soldiers lived and fought in these filthy trenches, in the company of rotting corpses and rats. They were ordered at intervals to climb 'over the top' and advance through the enemy's barbed wire. On just the first day of the Battle of the Somme, 19,000 men were killed and 57,000 were wounded. The horrendous death toll was increased by the epidemics of typhus, cholera and dysentery that swept through the trenches. Most soldiers had gone to the Front with a keen sense of patriotism. Many of the survivors, however, returned home in a state of despair.

Some of the women who went to the battle zone were equally appalled. Vera Brittain went as a nurse because, she said, 'not being a man and able to go to the Front, I wanted to do the next best thing.' She was horrified by what she saw. 'It is impossible,' she concluded, 'to find any satisfaction in the thought of . . . slaughtered Germans, left to mutilation and decay; the destruction of men as though beasts, whether they be English, French, German or anything else, seems a crime to the whole march of civilisation.' Brittain became a firm pacifist.

Before the outbreak of war, the women's movement had been united in the struggle for the vote. Now there was a split between women who supported the war and women who wanted

Neutrality League Announcement No. 2.

ENGLISHMEN, DO YOUR DUTY

And Keep Your Country Out of a

WICKED AND STUPID WAR.

Small but powerful cliques are trying to rush you into it. You must

DESTROY THE PLOT TO-DAY
or it will be too late.

Left *This anti-war statement in a daily newspaper shows how worried some people felt about Britain's preparations for war against Germany in 1914.*

peace. Many pacifists were convinced that if women were in the government, the war would not have started in the first place. Three days after the declaration of war, Harriette Beanland, a suffragist dressmaker in Lancashire, commented that, '[There is an] erroneous impression that this and other countries are at war with one another. They are not. Their governments, composed of men and responsible only to the men of each country, and backed by the majority of men who have caught the war and glory fever, have declared war on one another.' She added that, 'The women of all these countries have not been consulted as to whether they would have war or not . . . '

Sylvia Pankhurst, a suffragette in the Women's Social and Political Union (WSPU), maintained that the war was a 'huge and shameful loss to humanity'. Emmeline Pethick-Lawrence, also in the WSPU, travelled around the USA to raise support for reconciliation with Germany. Many of the different suffragist societies pleaded with the government to remain neutral and to pull back from war. All these women supported the No-Conscription Fellowship, which was set up to help conscientious objectors when conscription was introduced in 1916.

Sylvia Pankhurst's sister Christabel, and her mother Emmeline, condemned any opposition to the war. They themselves were enthusiastic about it. 'This was national militancy,' said Christabel. 'As Suffragettes,' she explained, 'we could not be pacifists at any price. We offered our service to the country and called upon all our members [of the WSPU] to do likewise.' At her first public appearance in Britain following the declaration of war, she was billed to speak on 'The Great Need Of Vigorous National Defence Against The German Peril'.

For Christabel and Emmeline Pankhurst, men in uniform were heroes. By the same token, men who did not want to fight were cowards. Emmeline even went round the country handing out white feathers, a symbol of cowardice, to young men in civilian clothes. She and Christabel supported military

6

I could not give my name to aid the slaughter in this war, fought on both sides for grossly material ends, which did not justify the sacrifice of a single mother's son. Sylvia Pankhurst, *The Home Front*, 1932.

9

Above *Sylvia Pankhurst condemned Britain's entry into the First World War and actively campaigned for peace. This opposition to the war irritated her mother and sister, who were also suffragettes but had a keen sense of patriotism.*

Right *Christabel Pankhurst, who travelled round the country with her mother in an effort to recruit men to the forces. They also organized demonstrations urging women to do war work at home.*

conscription for men. They were infected by the anti-German feeling that was spreading through the country and wanted Germans in Britain to be put in prison. 'Intern them all,' cried Emmeline. The *Suffragette,* the journal of the WSPU in the days of the suffragette movement, reappeared as a pro-war paper called the *Britannia.*

There were posters everywhere recruiting men to join the forces. The poster declaring that 'Women of Britain say – "Go"' shows a mother and her children gazing with admiration at the passing backs of a troop of marching soldiers. Its message is that men go to war to protect their families and homes, and that women should encourage their sacrifice. Certainly, many young women did. Siegfried Sassoon, a poet who fought in the trenches, was troubled by the idea that women thought about the soldiers in this way. In 'Glory of Women', a poem he wrote in 1917, he complained to women that:

> 'You love us when we're heroes, home on leave,
> Or wounded in a mentionable place.
> You worship decorations; you believe
> That chivalry redeems the war's disgrace.
> You make us shells. You listen with delight,
> By tales of dirt and danger fondly thrilled.
> You crown our distant ardurs while we fight,
> And mourn our laurelled memories when we're killed.
> You can't believe that British troops 'retire'
> When hell's last horror breaks them, and they run,
> Trampling the terrible corpses – blind with blood.'

' *. . . it is we who 'mother the men' who have to uphold the honour and traditions not only of our Empire but of the whole civilised world . . . We women . . . will tolerate no such cry as Peace! Peace! where there is no peace . . . We women pass on the human ammunition of 'only sons' to fill up the gaps . . .* From a letter in the London *Morning Post,* 1916, signed 'A Little Mother'. '

3

Women in Uniform

1914–1918

The chief role of women at the Front during the First World War was that of caring for the sick and wounded. Sixty years before, Florence Nightingale had given respectability to the idea of women nurses in the combat zone. Now, nurses were encouraged to join the war effort as VADs (members of the Voluntary Aid Detachment). Women doctors were not so welcome. The War Office told Dr Elsie Inglis, who had the backing of the Scottish Suffrage Societies to equip an all-woman medical unit, to 'go home and sit still'. Inglis did not sit still, but offered her units to the other Allied forces. By the end of the war there were fourteen Scottish Women's Hospital units attached to every Allied force – except the British!

Perhaps the most famous nurse of the First World War was Edith Cavell, whose courage and determination led people to question the common view that women were fragile and dependent. At the outbreak of war, she was the director of a school of nursing in Brussels, the capital of Belgium. Her hospital was converted into a Red Cross Hospital, to care for the wounded of all nationalities. Although Cavell was committed to the care of all, whether friend or foe, she also assisted in the escape of Allied soldiers caught behind enemy lines. She knew that in

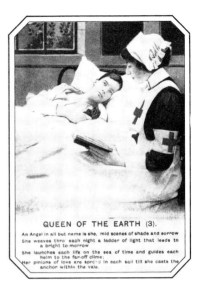

QUEEN OF THE EARTH (3).

An Angel in all but name is she, mid scenes of shade and sorrow
She weaves thro each night a ladder of light that leads to a bright to-morrow
She launches each life on the sea of time and guides each helm to the far-off clime;
Her pinions of love are spread in each sail till she casts the anchor within the vale.

Above *The nurse on this postcard looks rather like an angel. This was a popular image of nurses during the First World War.*

> *The patients are sleeping out now, in the cloisters at the back of the Abbey . . . They sent word from Creil [a nearby town] that we might be having a lot in at any time of the day or night. I do not smoke much, Mother, only a little to soothe my nerves.* From a letter home by a nurse working for a Scottish Women's Hospital in France in 1915.

> *Standing as I do in view of God and Eternity, I realize that patriotism is not enough. I must have no hatred or bitterness towards anyone.* Edith Cavell, just before she was shot by the Germans in 1915.

Left *Edith Cavell, who helped Allied soldiers to escape from the enemy while she was matron of a hospital in Brussels. She was eventually caught by the Germans and shot.*

doing so she was risking her life, as Brussels was under German military law. In 1915, Cavell was arrested by the Germans and was executed by a firing squad.

Two British women set up a First Aid Post at the Front in the Belgian sector. They remained there until they were both gassed, early in 1918. Although military hospitals were usually at a little distance from the fighting, all the female staff were exposed to attack from the enemy, especially when working on hospital ships.

The women also had to cope daily with the sight of dead, dying and mutilated bodies. Vera Brittain described the horror she witnessed as a VAD: 'The enemy within shelling distance – refugee Sisters crowding in with nerves all awry – bright moonlight, and aeroplanes carrying machine-guns – ambulance trains jolting noisily into the siding, all day, all night – gassed men on stretchers, clawing the air – dying men, reeking with mud and foul green-stained bandages, shrieking and writhing in a grotesque travesty of manhood – dead men with fixed, empty eyes and shiny, yellow faces . . .'

The role of volunteer women in the war zone was not limited to the care of the wounded. The First Aid Nursing Yeomanry (FANY) had a clear policy (despite their name!) of leaving the task of nursing to other groups of women. They provided transport where necessary, taking considerable risks as ambulance

The First Aid Nursing Yeomanry (FANY) had the reputation of looking smart. These ambulance drivers are wearing fur coats over their khaki uniform while on duty in France.

drivers and despatch riders. By the end of the war there were 116 FANYs working in France under the auspices of the Red Cross. They prided themselves on their smart appearance, and some of them wore fur coats over their khaki uniforms!

Most of the volunteers received no pay in the first half of the war. This meant that women from the working classes could not join up. Some women even had to pay for their uniform! The uniform of the Women's Volunteer Reserve (khaki coat, skirt and felt hat, with shoes and puttees) cost £2.10s, which was beyond the reach of most women. By 1916, it was decided to pay VADs and other volunteers an annual salary of £20-30. This sum of money, though not large, soon boosted numbers. It also offered material proof that women were needed by the War Office.

An even stronger indication of women's importance in the war effort was the establishment of women's sections of the forces. By 1917, the Women's Army Auxiliary Corps (WAAC) employed 60,000 women, 10,000 of whom went to France. The Women's Royal Naval Service (WRNS) replaced on land the men who went to fight at sea, and in 1918 the Women's Royal Air Force (WRAF) developed from the women's arm of the Royal Flying Corps. The chief task of these servicewomen was to support the male forces. Only one woman, Flora Sandes, actually bore arms against the enemy.

Below Members of the Women's Royal Air Force waiting to be flown to Germany.

Flora Sandes (1876–1956)

Flora Sandes was the only British woman to fight as a soldier on the battlefields of the First World War. In 1914, when she was thirty-eight, she went to Serbia to work as a nurse in a Red Cross ambulance unit. When the Serbs were driven back by the Bulgarian Army, Sandes refused to leave them and joined the retreat. They soon reached mountainous country that could not be passed in an ambulance, so she enlisted as a soldier. Since more than half of the 800,000 who set out on the retreat did not survive it, Sandes was fortunate not to die on the way. She is said to have raised the spirits of the other soldiers by playing the violin that she always had with her.

In 1916, when the Serbs were breaking through the Bulgarian front, Flora found herself in the thick of battle. There was 'Incessant fighting [and] weariness indescribable,' she wrote in her autobiography, adding that it was 'hand-in-hand with romance, adventure and comradeship.' At last the Bulgarians were driven back. But during an attack on a strategic hill top, Flora was hit by a grenade and was taken to a Scottish Women's Hospital. Her bravery was rewarded by the Kara-George Star, the most coveted decoration in the army. After a long spell in hospital, Sandes joined the bitter fighting that led to the Serbs' eventual victory over the enemy. British troops participated in the final attack but made no mention of Flora's courage. In Serbia, on the other hand, she became a legend.

Sergeant Major Flora Sandes, the only British woman to fight alongside men during the First World War. She was awarded a rare decoration for bravery.

Sandes remained on active service until 1922 and married a Russian *emigré* officer who had been in her regiment. They lived in France and then in Belgrade, where they were interned by the Germans during the Second World War. Sandes continued to live in Belgrade for a few years after her husband's death in 1941. She then went home to England, where she lived quietly for the rest of her extraordinary life.

4

War Work at Home

1914–1918

Life in wartime Britain was hard. On top of the depressing news in the casualty lists from the Front, there was the difficulty of daily existence. Food shortages soon developed, which led to queues. Lights were dimmed in towns and cities, newspapers were censored, and there was no room for any kind of luxury.

Working-class women suffered the most. Soldiers' wives got a meagre allowance from the state, and illegitimate war-babies were not provided for. To help the poor in London's East End, Sylvia Pankhurst set up a chain of cost-price restaurants and welfare centres for mothers and infants. She also established a toy factory to create work for unemployed women and girls, and converted a pub into a clinic, day nursery and school.

As the war continued, women in Britain were called upon to fill the jobs of servicemen and to produce weapons for the troops, especially after conscription for men was introduced in January 1916. There was quite a lot of public resistance to the idea of women working, which made the minister of munitions

Above *This woman took over her husband's chimney-sweep business while he was at the Front.*

Left *Children waiting for a free meal. Life was so hard for the poor during the First World War that many children relied on free food for their survival.*

'
There were women of all classes – ladies of title, working women and, in the majority, women and girls of the middle class – all eager, as the battle-cry of one of their hundred banners had it, to 'work, work, work'. The Observer, 18 July 1915, on the Women's Right-to-Serve Procession organized by the WSPU.
'

feel anxious about supplies for the Front. Christabel Pankhurst and the Women's Social and Political Union then organized a huge demonstration to recruit women to the war effort. The marchers carried banners with such messages as 'Shells Made By a Wife May Save a Husband's Life' and 'For Men Must Fight And Women Must Work'.

The trade unions did not want women to join the work-force. They complained that women were unskilled and that the cheapness of their labour would lower men's wages and threaten their job security. The government and employers promised that men would have their jobs back as soon as the war was over. The Unions then agreed to allow 'dilution' – that meant splitting up the work of a skilled man among several unskilled women.

Women worked in mills, breweries, refineries, tanneries, textiles, the postal and police services, the civil service, shipyards, coalfields and bakeries. They became mechanics, window cleaners, sweeps, carpenters, bus and tram conductors and drivers. In fact, they did just about everything that men had done before they left for the Front!

It is sometimes thought that the First World War 'liberated' women from the home and introduced them to the stimulation of the public world. To some extent this was true, especially for the women in the middle and upper classes who were given challenging jobs. For the first time, they earned an income and enjoyed a measure of independence. Domestic servants, too, welcomed the demands of wartime. They preferred work in the munitions factories, where they had some independence

A woman worker performs the vital job of constructing an aeroplane propeller in 1914. The fact that so many women contributed to victory challenged the traditional view of women as fragile and dependent.

and the company of other women, to their lonely and underpaid jobs in other people's homes. About 400,000 women left domestic service to join the war effort.

But for women who were already working in the factories and industry, nothing really changed. The outbreak of war did not bring relief from back-breaking work. They were still paid less than men for doing the same work, and it was still as difficult as before to be a working mother. Some crèches were set up to help working mothers, but too few to make much of a difference.

Work in the munitions factories, which produced military supplies such as weapons and ammunition, was exhausting. The working day for munitions workers was split into two twelve-hour shifts. Before the war, the Factory Acts had limited the hours of work to ten and a half per day, but munitions shifts were lengthened to meet the requirements of war. Work with the explosives was also dangerous. Prolonged exposure to TNT, a vital ingredient in munitions, caused toxic jaundice.

These women are filling shells in a munitions factory. Munitions workers were known as 'canary girls', because their skin was sometimes turned yellow by the material in explosives.

Members of the Women's Land Army collecting apples. These women look cheerful, but many WLAs were exhausted at the end of a long day of hard work.

6

. . . there were hearty and general cheers . . . It [marked] Parliament's appreciation of the splendid services of women in the war. Parliament's reaction in 1918 to the vote for women over thirty.

9

6

The idea that because the State called for women to help the nation, the State must continue to employ them is too absurd for serious women to entertain. As a matter of grace, notice should be at least a fortnight and if possible a month. *The Daily Graphic, 1918.*

9

This disease, which turned the women's skin yellow and gave them the name 'canary girls', was sometimes fatal. By the end of the war, 300 munitions women had been killed by TNT poisoning or by explosions at work.

Over 113,000 women served in the Women's Land Army (WLA) during the First World War. They kept the farms going and helped to grow the nation's food. Many women, especially those who had grown up in the cities, were attracted by the idea of a healthy life in the open air. Some Land Girls enjoyed themselves, but others were disappointed. The working day was often long, lonely and boring.

By the end of the First World War, women had a much more positive image of themselves. They knew that their part in the war had contributed to victory. Men knew this, too, and some admitted it. 'During this war,' remarked the prime minister in 1916, 'the women of this country have rendered as effective service in the prosecution of the war as any other class of the community.' If the franchise were to be extended to greater numbers of men, he said, then women had an 'unanswerable' case for getting it too. In 1918, most women over the age of thirty won the vote. Ten years later, every woman had the vote.

The changes in the daily life of women were unfortunately only temporary. As soon as the war was over, men went back to their jobs and most women were forced to return to their domestic routines.

5

Ireland

1880–1922

After the terrible suffering of the Irish famine in the late 1840s, more bad harvests in 1879 prompted Michael Davitt, joined by Charles Parnell, to set up the Land League to agitate for more control and security for tenants over their land. Fanny and Anna Parnell organized the Ladies Land League, to help them resist the eviction and rack-renting of peasants. This kind of supportive role was characteristic of the part played by women in Ireland's struggle for independence from Britain. Only a few women, such as Constance Markievicz, joined the leadership.

In 1913, the Irish Volunteers was formed as a military organization to fight for Ireland's independence from Britain. In the following year, a women's arm of the Volunteers was set up – the Cumann na mBan, or Irish Women's Council. Only women of Irish birth or descent were allowed to join. The Cumann issued a manifesto stating that, 'We are the only Women's Organisation belonging to the Irish Volunteers, and our activities and aims are solely National'. A member of the Cumann observed that, 'Everything was put aside and we were ready to do what we were told: carry messages, give first aid, make meals, in short any work.' Some women took part in gun-running, which was risky since the British had prohibited the import of arms into Ireland.

When war broke out between Britain and Germany in 1914, the Bill for Irish Home Rule was shelved. This added fuel to the nationalist cause, as did the long list from the Front of Irish casualties. More and more women joined the Cumann na mBan, which opposed Irish involvement in Britain's war. In 1914, the Cork branch of Cumann na mBan declared that it 'recognise[d] that our duty in the present crisis is to Ireland and Ireland alone'.

'We knew that there would be a Rising', wrote a member of the Cumann, but wondered 'what time, where, how?' The rising against the British finally happened in 1916 on Easter Monday. A small army of Republicans marched into the centre of Dublin and stopped at the General Post Office. They made the clerks and customers leave, and occupied the building. With

Above *Women in the Ladies Land League at work in the Dublin office. The Parnell sisters set up the Ladies Land League so that women could help in the struggle against the eviction of peasants from their homes.*

❝ *We call on all Irishwomen who realise that our National honour and our National needs must be placed before all other considerations, to join our ranks and give us all the assistance in their power.* From the Manifesto of the Cumann na mBan, 1914. **❞**

Some of Dublin was reduced to ruins by the Easter Rising of 1916. The Irish republicans held Dublin for almost a week, but were eventually crushed by British troops.

little more than 1,500 soldiers, they took control of several buildings in central Dublin and a few other places in the country. Constance Markievicz was the second in command.

The British attacked with force. The Volunteers managed to keep control of Dublin for nearly a week, but finally surrendered and were arrested. By this time, the centre of Dublin was in ruins. Sixteen of the leaders were shot by the British, and Markievicz was put in prison.

The Easter Rising was the beginning of a new era in the nationalist struggle. W.B. Yeats wrote in his poem *Easter 1916* that, 'A terrible beauty is born'. The insurgents had been showered with insults and rotten vegetables by Dubliners as they were led away by the British, but when the survivors of Easter week were released from prison they were given an enthusiastic welcome by the public. The martyrdom of the leaders of the Rising had won people over to the nationalist cause.

When the British tried to introduce military conscription in Ireland in 1918, they lost what was left of Irish support. People asked why they should fight for the rights of small countries like Belgium and Serbia, when Britain was not ready to give them their independence. If they were going to fight against anyone, said some, then it would be against the British.

The Anglo-Irish War of 1919–21 soon followed. When a Republican parliament was set up by Sinn Fein in 1919, it demanded the 'evacuation of our country by the English garrison,' and an end to British plans to partition the island. The British did not agree and a guerrilla war ensued, in which the Cumann took an active part. They undertook a variety of dangerous tasks, including dispatch-carrying, intelligence work and first aid, often in high-risk zones. Several women were wounded and others served jail sentences.

When the war came to an end, it was reported that there were nearly 800 branches of the Cumann in Ireland as well as in England and Scotland. Following the official independence of Eire in 1922, a member of the Cumann wrote that the women of Ireland were 'unsung [and] unrecorded', but 'the heroines of history'.

A grief-stricken crowd, largely made up of women, stands outside a prison in Dublin in 1921, where Irish nationalists were about to be executed by the British.

Constance Markievicz (1868–1927)

Constance Markievicz is one of the few women to have fought on equal terms with men in the struggle to free Ireland from British control. She was born Constance Gore Booth, the eldest daughter of an Anglo-Irish landowner, and grew up in County Sligo. During the troubles of the 1880s, the sight of peasants being evicted from their cottages led her to become a member of Sinn Fein.

Constance went to Paris in 1898 to study painting. There she married Count Markievicz, a Pole, and they had a daughter. They divided their time between Poland and Ireland. In Dublin, she became a noted orator and leader in the nationalist movement. She organized a soup kitchen for the workers during the strikes of 1913. When the First World War broke out in 1914, she said at a public meeting that women were learning to shoot so that they could help resist conscription.

In the Easter Rising of 1916, Markievicz was second in command of the Republican troops. Wearing a green uniform with breeches, she marched at the head of 120 soldiers to defend the park called St Stephen's Green against the British. When they had to surrender after three days of fighting, she took her revolver from its holster and kissed it. She then presented it to the astonished British officer and announced, 'I am ready'.

All the leaders of the rebellion were sentenced to death, but because Markievicz was a woman her sentence was commuted to life imprisonment. She was released in 1917 in an amnesty for Irish prisoners. The Irish

Countess Constance Markievicz, a leader in Ireland's struggle for independence from the British. She played an active role in the Easter Rising of 1916.

poet W.B. Yeats included Markievicz in his list of the rebellion's leaders in his poem *Easter 1916*.

So popular was Markievicz with the people of Ireland that she was elected to the House of Commons in 1918, despite the fact that she was back in prison at the time! She was the first woman to be elected to the British Parliament. Like other members of Sinn Fein, however, she refused to accept her seat as a matter of principle.

Markievicz was a vigorous supporter of the Republican government set up by Sinn Fein in 1919, and was made minister of labour. She was also an elected member of the Irish Parliament, following the official independence of Eire in 1922. After her death, a speech at her funeral declared that she was 'mourned by the people whose liberties she fought for; blessed by the loving prayers of the poor she tried so hard to befriend'.

6

The Spanish Civil War

1936–1939

In 1936, General Franco led a military uprising against Spain's Republican government, which had been legally and democratically elected. The Republicans fought back and the bitter Spanish Civil War began. Franco and his followers were fascists. They did not respect democratic institutions and were prepared to go to any lengths to take power. Fascists are typically racist, nationalistic and aggressive towards other nations.

Many people in Britain supported the Republicans. They were worried by Franco's gangster behaviour and could see that he was part of a larger European fascist movement. In Italy, the fascist political party that had seized power in 1922 had eliminated any opposition to its leader, Mussolini. In Germany, Hitler was in the process of getting rid of all other political parties and destroying the trade unions.

Clearly any attempt to build a barrier to fascism was of international importance. Because of this, many people who had previously been opposed to war supported the resistance of the Republicans. 'Up till now a pacifist in the fullest sense', wrote Rosamond Lehmann, 'I have come to feel that non-resistance can be – in this case, is – a negative, sterile, even a destructive thing.'

Above *Nan Green, who risked her life in the front lines of the Spanish Civil War. This photograph shows her working for the National Joint Committee for Spanish Relief after her return to England.*

> *As a mother, I am convinced that upon the outcome of the struggle in Spain depends the future, the very life of my children.* Rosamond Lehmann, 1937.

Left *This ambulance is going to Spain to help casualties of the Spanish Civil War. Medical supplies of all kinds, as well as doctors and nurses, were sent to Spain by British opponents of Franco.*

Right *Many people in Britain supported the Republican government of Spain in its fight against fascism. In this photograph, women are collecting money in London for the Republican cause.*

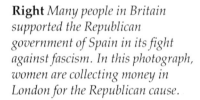

This hideous war, which is murdering Spain and may let war loose again over the whole of Europe, is the deliberate act of the two fascist dictators, and avowed by them as such. It is an act they will not hesitate to repeat. Storm Jameson in 1937.

Thousands of people went to Spain to take part in the war against fascism. They were formed into International Brigades, which fought alongside the Spanish Brigades. The International Brigades were chiefly composed of men. The women who supported the Spanish Republic tended to stay in their own country and organize fund-raising. They shipped medicines and books (especially books on Spanish grammar!) to the wounded in Spain, and they organized the evacuation of Spanish children to Britain.

There were some women, however, among the 2,000 British combatants. In fact, the first British volunteer to be killed by Franco's troops was a woman. She was Felicia Browne, an artist who had gone to Spain to draw and paint. She joined the militia in Barcelona on 2 August 1936, and was shot on 25 August

Right *Refugee children in Spain. They are being examined by English doctors and nurses before their departure for safety in England.*

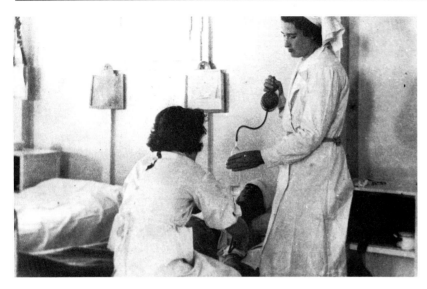

A British nurse and an American nurse taking care of a casualty of the Spanish Civil War.

while rescuing a friend who had been wounded on patrol.

Most of the women in the International Brigades did not take part in combat but served as drivers, nurses and administrators. They often found themselves in the sole company of men and longed to spend some time with women. After Nan Green, a nurse, had left the Front, she recalled the 'sudden surprise and delight I felt as we drove through our first village on the far side, to see women in the streets! I hadn't seen another woman for weeks, and wished I could get down and embrace them.' Green's work was varied. She had to organize the casualty lists and classify them into various categories – 'head wounds, leg wounds, amputations and so on'. She also gave blood. 'Being fortunate to be a Universal Donor,' she wrote, 'I was recruited to give some of my blood by direct transfusion . . . Lying down beside a seriously wounded man, on the point of death, I watched as the colour came back into his lips, his breathing improved and he turned back towards life.'

Franco defeated the Republic in 1939. For the people of Spain and the international volunteers, it could be said that the Second World War started in 1936. Looking back, the Spanish Civil War looks like a rehearsal before the big showdown against the fascists in Germany and Italy. Franco's troops and their German backers treated Spanish civilians with a barbaric cruelty that would soon be associated with fascism by most people in Europe. One nurse who witnessed some of the violence wrote that, 'In one instance, there was a deep chasm with a river winding through it outside the town of Cuenca, near where I had been stationed. The fascists filled that chasm with people and then machine-gunned them to death.'

> **. . . as a woman, I have no country. As a woman I want no country. As a woman my country is the whole world.**
> Virginia Woolf, *Three Guineas*, 1938.

Above *In the Second World War, bombing raids put civilians at as much risk as the fighting troops.*

6

Our vicar, an elderly man who had been shell-shocked in the trenches in the last war, mounted the pulpit and said, in a voice that was almost inaudible, 'We are now at war with Germany. We will return to our homes'. One woman's memory of the day when Britain declared war on Germany in 1939.

9

6

Before the war I hadn't been too keen on women's company. I came away from the camps liking women and respecting their resource. A comment by a woman who survived a Japanese internment camp.

9

7

The Second World War

1939–1945

The Second World War began when Adolf Hitler's Nazi forces invaded Poland in 1939, after many months of threatening behaviour all over Europe. Britain and France declared war to support Poland. During the course of the war, the Nazis occupied many countries, including Denmark, Norway, Holland, Belgium and parts of France. They also invaded part of Russia. Germany's supporters included the fascist regimes in Italy and Spain, and also Japan, which wanted to expand its empire in Asia. Britain was one of the forty-nine Allies that fought against them.

In the First World War, most of the casualties were men who had fought in the trenches. But in this war, the victims were civilians and troops alike. In Britain, the civilian population was the target of bombing raids. Between September 1940 and May 1941, the *Luftwaffe*, the German Air Force, dropped 55,305 tonnes of bombs on Britain. In the occupied countries, civilians had to cope with the presence of the enemy on a daily basis. In Soviet Russia, which was invaded by the German army but not defeated, at least 20 million civilians were killed. In Leningrad alone, more than a third of its 3 million inhabitants died of starvation before the German siege of the city was lifted.

About 20,000 British civilians living in South-East Asia were put in prison camps by the Japanese following the fall of Singapore, Malaya and the Dutch East Indies (which are now part of Indonesia). When the Japanese invaded, the British, Dutch and other foreigners tried to escape by ship, but many of the ships were captured or sunk. The women and their children were interned separately from the men. Unlike the men, as most of the women had not held positions of authority, they were not usually interrogated.

In most camps the women organized themselves to share the necessary tasks, such as cooking, cleaning, emptying the cesspits, and caring for the sick. 'Within a few days of internment,' writes one former internee, 'we organized ourselves as best we could. Some women cleaned rooms, some went on

duty to help prepare vegetables for the midday meal, and I started a school as the children rapidly got out of hand.' Another woman claims that while she was interned, she 'learnt that women can be very brave, very tenacious. If it had not been for that,' she adds, 'we would not be here now.'

Conditions in the camps were dreadful: they were over-crowded, and the food was insufficient and not very nutritious. The water was often contaminated, which in some cases led to constant dysentery. Facilities for washing were limited, and there was little relief from the heat and the blaze of the sun. The internees were frequently ill, and about one third of the women did not survive the war.

Nazi Germany was fighting not simply to extend its frontiers, it also had a more sinister agenda – to spread and to carry out the principles of fascism. The Nazis believed they were some kind of 'master race', and that Jews were an inferior race that should be exterminated. By 1942, the Nazis had murdered thousands of Jews in Poland and Russia. Jews in Germany and the occupied countries were made to wear yellow stars to iden-tify themselves; they lost their businesses and jobs.

Then things got even worse. The Nazi leaders decided to

Above *Women prisoners preparing food at a Japanese internment camp in Batavia. Survivors have recalled the way in which the women's efforts to share tasks and difficulties made life in captivity easier to bear.*

'
In Tangarang [prison] we got our water from two taps in the main compounds, and it was necessary to filter it through a bit of rag to get rid of the larger worms, with which the water seethed. One woman's memory of internment in Java during the Second World War.
'

Right *A waxwork image of Anne Frank writing her famous diary while in hiding. Her family had to shelter from the Germans because they were Jewish. They were eventually caught and died in concentration camps.*

‘ ━━━━━━━━━━

The emancipation of women is only an invention of the Jewish intellect. Adolf Hitler.

━━━━━━━━━━ ’

make the extermination of Jews 'scientific', devising the 'Final Solution'. Jews were rounded up and taken by train to death camps. These camps, such as Auschwitz, Treblinka, Belzec, and Chelmno, contained gas chambers in which to kill the prisoners, and a crematorium to burn their bodies. Of the Jews who went to the camps, 2 per cent were selected for slave labour. All the rest – at least 6 million – were killed. Other so-called 'asocials', including gypsies, homosexuals and communists, were also murdered in the death camps.

Anne Frank was a young Jewish girl whose family fled from Germany to Amsterdam in 1933. During the Nazi occupation of Holland, she and her family hid in a concealed part of her father's office. She kept a careful diary during the last two years of her short life. *Diary of a Young Girl* reveals the horror of living as a Jew under the threat of the Nazis. 'Surely the time will come when we are people again,' she wrote, 'and not just Jews'. She also wrote of the experiences shared by most adolescent girls: her first kiss, and her irritation with her mother. In 1944, when Anne was fifteen, she and her family were discovered by the Nazis and were taken to a death camp. Most of the family were gassed, and Anne and her sister died from typhus.

The horror of fascism challenged many people's opposition to war. Vera Brittain, who had been converted to pacifism by her experience as a VAD in the First World War, was one of the very few people to question publicly the British government's policy of fighting until there was an 'unconditional surrender' by the Germans. For most women and men in Britain, the Second World War was a 'just' war – a necessary fight against evil.

8

Women on Active Service

1939–1945

Women played an 'auxiliary' role in the services. This means that they were supposed to be helping the men, but not actually fighting. The job of women, it was said, was that of 'freeing the men for action'. This notion is reflected in the names of some of the women's forces – the Auxiliary Territorial Service (ATS), which 'helped' the Army, and the Women's Auxiliary Air Force (WAAF), which 'helped' the RAF.

The notion that women could serve in the armed forces without actually fighting, was not always a straightforward one. During the war, Churchill encouraged the anti-aircraft commander to form anti-aircraft batteries composed of both men and women. The commander did so, but made sure that only the men were 'combatants'. He assigned men to the guns, and women to fire-control, searchlight operations, targeting and hit confirmation. But, of course, women and men were equally at risk from attack by enemy bombs and fighters!

The tasks of women in the forces were varied. During the evacuation of the British Army at Dunkirk in France, ATS telephonists remained in Paris until they were among the last Allied

Above *Women on duty in an anti-aircraft battery.*

6

You know, on the anti-aircraft units, the ATS girls are never allowed to fire the guns . . . If girls fired guns, and women generals planned the battles . . . then men would feel there was no morality to war. They would have no one to fight for, nowhere to leave their consciences . . . Ian McEwan, *The Imitation Game*, 1981.

9

Left *During air raids, women in the Auxiliary Territorial Service (ATS) plotted the course of enemy raiders and relayed this information to the defence services. The ATS women in this photograph are being instructed in the skills of 'plotting'.*

Odette Churchill (on the left) and Marjorie Smith, two British agents who survived their dangerous work behind enemy lines in occupied France. Churchill had been caught and tortured by the Gestapo, but did not give away any information that might endanger other agents.

troops to leave the French capital. They actually drove their truck out of Paris as the Germans marched in on the other side of the city. Some of the women in the Women's Army Auxiliary Corps were 'Hush-WAACs', which meant that they worked in intelligence. In 1944, for ten days before D-Day, ATS soldiers baked bread that would not go stale for the invasion force. In every branch of the forces, there were women working in technical areas like radio and radar. Their competence showed how foolish was the belief that only men could learn technical skills.

Most of the nursing of the troops was done by women. Some of these nurses, in particular those with the Air Ambulance Service, crossed enemy lines to rescue the wounded. One of the first nurses to fly in this service remembers that, 'We dodged in and out of bombs, picked up the wounded [from North-West Europe] and brought them back to England. We were able to see the most horrific things and the next minute turn round and weep with laughter. We lived for the day; we had to grab our happiness as we could.'

The bravest people in the war included the women who carried out secret missions for the Resistance, which was an underground organization in France that fought against the German occupation. The British women who were chosen for this dangerous work were usually fluent in French and familiar with some region in occupied France. They knew that if they were caught by the Gestapo, the Nazi police, they faced torture and certain death.

These heroines included Noor Inayat Khan and Violette Szabo, both of whom were sent to France by the British Special Operations Executive (SOE). Szabo had to instruct Resistance groups on plans to attack German strongholds, so that the Allied landings in Normandy would have a better chance of success. She was captured by the Gestapo, tortured, and finally executed at Ravensbruck, the women's death camp. The citation announcing the posthumous award of her George Cross stated that, 'She was continuously and atrociously tortured but never by word or deed gave anything of any value . . . [She] gave a magnificent example of courage and steadfastness.'

When men came home at the end of the war, they were received as heroes and found work almost as soon as they took off their uniforms. But women got little recognition for their part in the war and had trouble finding civilian jobs. 'I remember when I was de-mobbed,' recalls one woman who was a wireless operator in the ATS. 'It felt like an empty stretch ahead of you. No one today seems to have any memory of us and the work we did.'

Noor Inayat Khan (1914–1944)

Noor Inayat Khan was the first woman radio operator to be infiltrated into enemy-occupied France during the Second World War. Born in Moscow to a wealthy Indian father and an American mother, she spent the First World War in Britain. The family lived in France while she was a teenager, but they were forced to return to Britain by the German invasion of France in 1940. Noor then enlisted in the Women's Auxiliary Air Force (WAAF).

Because of her fluency in French and her knowledge of France, she was soon referred to the Special Operations Executive (SOE). In 1942, she volunteered for training as a secret agent specializing in radio work, which had been her trade in the WAAF. One night in 1943, she was flown to France to be a wireless operator in one of the leading Resistance groups in the Paris area. For three and a half months, she carried out her mission, constantly at risk of being discovered by the Germans. The entire German intelligence network in the area was looking out for this brave woman, who was known only by her code name of 'Madeleine'. She was finally betrayed and captured.

The Germans had found Khan's codes and would have been able to send false messages back to London, if Khan had agreed to help. But she refused. Despite torture, she did not give her captors any help or information at all. She was kept in solitary confinement for nine months, mostly in chains because she kept trying to escape. Her death came when she was taken with three other women in the Resistance to the Dachau death camp. They were forced to kneel down in the crematorium compound

Noor Inayat Khan, the British agent who carried out secret missions in occupied France under the code name of 'Madeleine'.

and were then shot in the back of the neck.

Khan was awarded the George Cross after her death. At a ceremony to remember her life and work, the comment was made that Noor Inayat Khan GC was 'one of the most splendid and gallant women in our history . . . she was always utterly staunch and true to the cause of freedom and to the comrades who were working with her.'

❝

Here in Dachau on the 12th of September 1944 four young Women Officers of the British Forces attached to Special Operations Executive (SOE) were brutally murdered and their bodies cremated. They died as gallantly as they had served the Resistance in France during the common struggle for freedom from tyranny. A tablet at the Dachau concentration camp, in memory of Noor Inayat Khan and three other women.

❞

..Shoot straight, Lady

ISSUED BY THE MINISTRY OF FOOD

Above *An information sheet distributed by the Ministry of Food in 1943. Its message to housewives is that serving a family with healthy food is a 'vital active part in the drive to Victory'.*

9

The Home Front

1939–1945

In a sense, the front line in the Second World War was everywhere. It was not confined to the trenches or to a combat zone where men were dressed as soldiers. Throughout the war, British civilians were at risk from air raids. They felt lucky if they emerged alive from their shelters at the end of a raid and if their homes were not bombed. Even babies were issued with

Right *This couple has just left the rubble of their London home, which was destroyed by a German bomb. They are using a baby's pram to move their few remaining possessions.*

gas masks, and the air raid sirens could go at any time of the day or night. One woman remembers that, 'we used to have to go down underground in one of those Anderson shelters. Sometimes you were down there for hours, listening to the drone of the planes. And then you'd come out and see the whole sky lit up. You'd think, "I wonder who's gone now?"'

The problems of the poor were made worse by war. The lack of a National Health Service (it was not set up until 1948) was felt more acutely, because the limited medical facilities that had been available were taken over by the armed forces. One woman who gave birth to her son in 1942 said that her stay in hospital was a 'nightmare'. The room she was in was not properly equipped because 'they'd commandeered most of the hospital for the wounded servicemen'. Every morning, she said, 'you got porridge, but it was like Polyfilla. You got a glass of milk which was sour, always, and a piece of bread curled up at the edges.' The hospital did not have nappies, and 'half the time [the babies] had old pieces of khaki round them . . . there was no skin on him at all, he was just like a piece of liver underneath.' On top of all these problems, mothers had to cope with the rationing of food and clothes.

The evacuation of city children to the countryside was an added worry. Mothers felt that they ought to send their children to safety, but missed them badly once they had gone. Of course, many children were glad to get away from the dangers of the city and enjoyed the pleasures of the fields, flowers and animals. One person remembers that, 'we frequently adapted very

> *Another blitzy night,*
> *We were in the shelter all right.*
> *Anti-aircraft guns waxed strong.*
> *Out there . . . all Hell*
> *Was loose, the night long.*
> From 'Flooded Shelter', by Violet Power *A Woman's War Poems.*

Left *Some of the first casualties of the Second World War, under the care of women nurses at a military hospital in England.*

quickly, taking part in a rural life much more open and eventful than it is today.' But some children pined for their families.

Children who were sent to Canada, the USA and Australia suffered the most from evacuation. One woman has felt unsettled ever since she was evacuated to Canada at the age of seven. 'Suddenly,' she explains, 'I was with a bunch of children; we were all bundled up together and shipped out, total strangers.' She did not like the Canadian couple that took her in and worried constantly that they would adopt her if her parents were killed. When she returned home to Britain at the end of the war, she felt uncomfortable there too: 'I had a funny accent – I was Canadian – and I really felt as if I were a stranger interrupting this family's life. I didn't seem to belong to them any more.'

As in the First World War, organizations like the Women's Land Army flourished and women filled the jobs that had been vacated by servicemen. But in this war, even more women were

Below *These children are waiting for a train to take them away from London, where they could be killed by bombs from enemy aircraft. Most evacuated children spent the years of war in the countryside.*

needed to produce a steady stream of supplies for the military forces. The factories had trouble keeping up with demand, which increased with every year of the war. After conscription for men was introduced in June 1939, the government called on women to volunteer for work. Too few responded, so in December 1941 the National Service (no. 2) Act was passed, making war work compulsory. All single women between the ages of eighteen and thirty were conscripted either into industry or into the armed forces. The government also lifted the marriage bar so that married women could join the work-force.

Fifteen hundred nurseries were set up to help these married women, and a few managers tried to fit shifts around school. Others let women do their shopping during lunch, and some shops stayed open for this purpose. Work places provided canteens, more schools provided lunches, and 2,000 British Restaurants were opened to offer inexpensive meals. But since 2 million married women were now at work (as well as the

Right *This woman's role in the war effort was to take care of children while their mothers were at work in the munitions factories.*

'
The average woman takes to welding as readily as she takes to knitting once she has overcome any initial nervousness due to sparks. Indeed the two occupations have much in common, since they both require a small, fairly complex manipulative movement which is repeated many times combined with a kind of sub-conscious concentration at which women excel. Wartime leaflet by the Ministry of Labour for the shipbuilding industry.
'

'
I cannot see women settling to trivial ways – women who have done worthwhile things. From *Nella's Last War: a mother's diary, 1939–45* (ed. Richard Broad and Suzie Fleming).
'

women who were not married, some of whom also had children), these provisions were inadequate. Many women still had to make their own arrangements and found it difficult to juggle the needs of home and the demands of work.

Peacetime brought redundancy for many of these women, as it did for the women in the forces. One woman pilot who had enjoyed her wartime job of transporting new aircraft, was keen to continue flying after the war, but 'there were no jobs for women pilots; there were too many ex-RAF pilots looking for jobs . . .' A woman in the shipyards was horrified to lose her job several months before the war ended. All twelve women welders lost their job on the same day, she says, even though 'there was plenty of work in the yard'.

At first, it seemed that women would return to their domestic routines just as they had after the First World War, but there were differences. For one thing, women gained a measure of freedom from the post-war provision of free health care and family allowances. Also, the marriage bar, which had stopped married women from working, was now seen as out-dated. However, women were still not paid as much as men. Even though women had shown in two world wars that they could work as well and as hard as men, it was not until 1970 that the Equal Pay Act was passed. This required women to be paid the same rates as men for the same kind of work, although it was not fully implemented until 1975.

10

Women and War Today

1950–1990

There is an absence of peace in Northern Ireland today that is characteristic of a war zone. Women are involved on every side of the conflict. There are women in the British Army and Royal Ulster Constabulary, who regularly have to search women and children in Belfast and at border checkpoints. There are also women civilians who resent the presence of the British Army in Northern Ireland.

Some Catholic and some Protestant women have taken part in the actions of paramilitary organizations, but most women are victims of the violence and want it to stop. One woman saw two men break into her home and kill her husband, who was a Republican sympathizer. She remembers that she was wounded and that:

> '. . . the baby was in hysterics. After the gunmen had left, my two girls came up behind me, screaming. My eldest girl, who was seven, has a very strong character. She kept saying, "Mummy, what can I do? What can I

Above *A woman weeps at the funeral of her husband, a constable in the Royal Ulster Constabulary (RUC) who was murdered by the Irish Republican Army (IRA).*

Women in the Irish Republican Army (IRA). One woman is standing guard with her revolver while the other takes aim with her rifle.

Above *Women in Ulster banging dustbin lids on the pavements to warn neighbours that British soldiers are nearby, and to distract the soldiers during their searches.*

do?" I tried to tell her to go and get help, but I had to say it three times before she understood what I was saying. Her father's body was lying half-way out the bedroom door and across the top of the stairs and she had to climb over it to get out.'

Another woman saw her Loyalist husband and their two children blown up by a bomb that had been set by the Republicans. On that dreadful day, she says:

'The car was right in front of the window when it exploded. The shock of the impact left me motionless, unable to see or hear anything, and it was only my child talking about the smoke and broken glass that made me realize what had happened. When I got outside the car was completely torn apart. My husband and daughter were still sitting in the front seat, but their legs were badly cut up and I thought they were unconscious. Richard was not in the car, and I realized he had been thrown out of it by the blast. He was lying across the road.'

She knows, she says, why the bombers murdered her husband. What she cannot understand is how or why they could bring themselves to kill her innocent children. 'But tell me,' she asks, '– what about my children?'

Mairead Corrigan and Betty Williams were awarded the Nobel Peace Prize in 1977 for their contribution to peace in Northern Ireland. Corrigan was the aunt of three children who were killed in 1976 by a car that went out of control when soldiers shot dead a member of the Irish Republican Army (IRA). Corrigan and Williams spoke publicly about their distress over the deaths of the children and about their opposition to the IRA. Within a few weeks, thousands of 'Peace People' had marched in demonstrations of support. Although the group eventually lost its momentum, it offered a sense of hope for a time because it did not identify itself with any one side and because it wanted a peaceful solution.

Outside Northern Ireland, most British women in the second half of the twentieth century have been spared the horrors of war. The war in the Falkland Islands against Argentina in 1982 was chiefly a men's affair. The involvement of women was limited to some nurses in the naval task force.

Some women, though, have gone out of their way to enter the combat zone of a foreign war. The surgeon Pauline Cutting and the nurse Susie Wighton, for example, risked their lives in the 1980s to give medical care to Palestinian refugees in Lebanon.

War correspondents have also been exposed to the dangers of war. Victoria Brittain's work as a foreign correspondent for television and the press took her to Vietnam in the early 1970s. She reported on the last years of American military involvement in Vietnam and described the suffering she saw in the orphanages and hospitals. She was on assignment in Uganda in 1979, when the Tanzanian army deposed Idi Amin; at the scene of the civil war in Eritrea in 1980; and went to Angola several times to report on the South African occupation.

Kate Adie is another foreign correspondent of the 1980s who has a reputation for being at the centre of the news. She witnessed the American bombing of Libya in 1987, providing full coverage for the BBC. She was in Afghanistan in 1989 when the Soviet troops were withdrawn, and she was in Tiananmen Square, Beijing, when rebel students were murdered, also in 1989. For her and for Brittain, a war zone is no more unsuitable for female than for male reporters.

Above *Kate Adie is often seen on television reporting 'live' from a war zone abroad.*

> *Wives and families – the ones they say it's all for – have never been taken into consideration, and never will be. War is a man's job in a man's world.*
> The reaction of a sailor's wife to the Navy during the Falklands War, 1982.

> *Before, I had just been a spectator of this war, now I was part of it.* Jillian Robertson, *Sunday Express*, about her experience of a bombing mission in South Vietnam in a B-57.

Pauline Cutting (b. 1952)

The British surgeon Pauline Cutting has been called a 'modern day Florence Nightingale'. In 1985, she went to Beirut to work in a Palestinian refugee camp called Bourj al Barajneh. Her contract was for three months, but she stayed for a year and a half.

During the last five months of Cutting's stay, the camp was besieged by the Lebanese Shiite Amal militia. They bombarded the camp with artillery and shot at anyone who tried to leave. As the siege continued, the already basic conditions in the camp became appalling. There was no running water, no electricity, and hardly any food. Mothers who left the camp to find food for their children were shot at and sometimes killed. Malnutrition and frostbite became common.

Cutting performed more than 500 operations during the siege, in a makeshift operating theatre. On one occasion, writes Cutting, 'As we finished operating on the first two casualties, a bomb landed on the path to the hospital. Two more people were killed and another four wounded. We ran to the emergency room in our blood-drenched gowns.' Medical supplies dwindled away, so blood-stained dressings were washed and re-used and local anaesthetics were used for minor operations.

Cutting managed to get a message out of the camp so that the world would know what was happening. The news was transmitted world-wide by the BBC and shocked people everywhere. The siege finally ended when the International Red Cross entered the camp.

After her return home, Cutting arranged for two small boys to be flown out of Beirut so that their bullet-shattered spines could be treated in England. Her book *Children of the Siege* is based on diaries she kept during her ordeal. She wrote it, she says, so that people would know about the suffering and the courage of the people in the camps. Cutting was awarded the OBE in 1987. She is now married to a Dutch nurse who was also working in Bourj al Barajneh camp during the siege. They both plan to work again in the Middle East.

Dr Pauline Cutting, the surgeon who risked her life by remaining in a besieged Palestinian refugee camp in Beirut, in order to care for the sick and wounded.

11

Working for a Future

The British forces are becoming more prepared to think of women as fighters. In 1981, the Air Force recommended that its women be issued with guns. The British Army, which has been actively recruiting women since the early 1970s, has stated that it too is ready to start training members of the Women's Royal Army Corps (WRAC) in the use of handguns.

Many women, however, do not regard the carrying of weapons as a sign of progress or of women's liberation. As long ago as 1739, a woman called Mary Wortley Montague claimed that women's disinterest in war made them superior to men. 'The real truth,' she said, '[is] that humanity and integrity, the characteristics of our sex, makes us abhor unjust slaughter, and prefer honourable peace to unjust war.' The same claim has been made today, but in different words. It is time, say some feminists, to 'take the toys from the boys'.

Above *Joan Ruddock, who was elected chairperson of the Campaign for Nuclear Disarmament (CND) in 1981. She continues to work for a nuclear-free world, both in her role as a Labour MP and as a concerned member of the public.*

Left *During the First and Second World Wars, women rarely carried guns. But in the 1980s, some women in the British forces began to be trained in the use of firearms. This member of the Women's Royal Army Corps (WRAC) is in the Women's Army rifle team.*

Dora Russell (on the left), who campaigned for peace throughout her life. She was active in the Campaign for Nuclear Disarmament (CND) and led the Women's Caravan of Peace across Europe in 1958 to protest against the Cold War.

The 'toys' of today are various and lethal: 'conventional' arms like machine-guns, chemical weapons, and nuclear bombs that can be launched by long-range missiles. Enough nuclear weapons now exist to destroy the world several times over. In a nuclear war, the question of whether or not women should be combatants would become irrelevant. Everyone would be a non-combatant. Everyone would be a victim. There would be no opportunity for heroism or even for any kind of resistance. When nuclear bombs were dropped on Hiroshima and Nagasaki at the end of the Second World War, the civilians could do nothing but suffer and die.

The largest British peace movement is the Campaign for Nuclear Disarmament (CND), which considers the existence of nuclear missiles to be a major threat to the survival of the human race. CND is made up of men as well as women, but women have influenced its direction. One woman who was especially powerful in CND from the 1950s was Dora Russell. In 1958, she led the Women's Caravan of Peace across Europe to protest against the Cold War that was dividing the USA and the USSR.

The Peace Camp at Greenham Common has been a powerful statement by British women of their objection to nuclear weapons. It started in 1981 as a non-violent protest against the proposed siting of Cruise missiles at the American Air Force base at Greenham. The missiles were installed in 1983, despite the attempts of the peace camp to obstruct the process. The women then worked together to monitor the 'secret' exercises of convoys of missiles outside the base.

Some women left their children in the care of fathers or friends in order to live at the camp. They were accused by the media and members of the public of not caring properly for their children. The Greenham women replied that it was precisely because they felt responsible for their children that they took this step. They have also defended their decision to keep men out of the camp by saying that it is 'a women's space in which to try to live out ideals of feminism and non-violence'.

In 1987, an agreement was made between the USA and the USSR that allowed for the removal of Cruise missiles from British bases. They have not yet been taken away from the Greenham base, but most of the women have left the camp and moved into other areas of the peace movement.

In times of war, British women have displayed courage, compassion and determination. In the First and Second World Wars, they showed they were equal to just about anything – and that any idea of male superiority over women was absurd. Women's

6

I've been accused of being cruel and hard-hearted for leaving my children behind, but it's exactly for my children that I'm doing this. In the past, men have left to go to war. Now women are leaving home for peace. Sarah Van Veen, Greenham woman, 1982.

9

6

. . . I need to know, tell me, how am I joined to the war machine, tell me

can I get off?
From 'Poem' by Janet Dube, in *Over our dead bodies* (ed. Dorothy Thompson).

9

Left *In the 1980s, many women lived in a peace camp outside the US Air Force base at Greenham Common. They were opposed to nuclear weapons and tried in many ways to obstruct the process of installing cruise missiles at the base. Here, some Greenham women who had been blocking the entrance to the base are dragged away by police.*

most significant achievement in the arena of war, however, is possibly their contribution to peace. In the last two centuries, many women have insisted that war is a foolish way to settle differences between nations. In the nuclear world of the late twentieth century, this insistence becomes more meaningful than it has ever been before. 'Perhaps it is the long unheard and ignored voices of women,' claimed Dora Russell in 1983, 'that may rescue the world in time from the nuclear madness which is absorbing all thought and action.'

Projects

1. Look at the posters on page 8 that were used in the First World War to recruit men to the armed forces. Try to find some more recruitment posters in books in your local library.

- What image of men do they convey?

- What image of women and their expectations of men is conveyed?
- Can you identify any particular details in the posters that contribute to their overall effect?
- What is your reaction to them?

---

2. Using a tape recorder, interview a woman in your family or your neighbourhood who lived through the Second World War. Decide ahead of time on the questions you want to ask, and write them down ready for use. If you can persuade a friend to do the same interview with another woman who lived through the war, you will be able to compare your answers. Here are some ideas for questions:

- What were your feelings when war was declared? Were you enthusiastic about it, opposed to it, or indifferent?
- Did your experience of the war change your first reaction to it?
- What did you do in the war? Were you evacuated/did you work in the factories/did you join the forces/did you take care of a family?

- Was anyone in your family killed or wounded in the war?
- How were you affected by the rationing of food and clothes? What did you feel about it?
- Do you think that the Second World War was different in any way from the First World War?
- What is your opinion about the development of nuclear weapons?
- Do you have any views on the peace movement?

When you have completed the interview, use the recording you have made to write up the answers. Compare your set of answers with the one obtained by your friend. Are there any big differences between the two sets? If so, can you explain them?

---

3. Try to imagine what your life would have been like if you had lived through the First World War. Would your experience have been determined by your gender? If so, how?

Next, try to guess what part you might have played in the Second World War. Would your part have been different if you had been of the opposite sex?

Now, imagine – if you can – how you would react if war were declared today. Think about the kind of war that would be fought and how you would be involved. Would your sex influence in any way your experience of the war?

Finally, think about the three wartime experiences that you have just imagined. Are there any major differences between them? If so, what conclusions can you draw from these differences?

Books to Read

Books for younger readers

Bielenberg, Christabel *Christabel: The Past is Myself* (Corgi, rpt. of 1968 edition)

Brittain, Vera *Testament of Youth* (Virago, rpt. of 1933 edition)

Brittain, Vera *Testament of a Peace Lover* ed. W. and A. Eden-Green (Virago, 1988)

Castle, Barbara *Sylvia and Christabel Pankhurst* (Penguin, 1987)

Condell, Diana and Jean Liddiard *Working for Victory? Images of Women in the First World War 1914–1918* (Routledge and Kegan Paul, 1987)

Cook, Alice and Gwyn Kirk *Greenham Women Everywhere* (Pluto Press, 1983)

Cutting, Pauline *Children of the Siege* (Pan, 1987)

Frank, Anne *Anne Frank's Diary*, with a Foreword by Storm Jameson (Vallentine, Mitchell, 1947)

Holdsworth, Angela *Out of the Doll's House, The Story of Women in the Twentieth Century* (BBC Books, 1988)

Jackson, Robert *Heroines of World War II* (Arthur Barker Ltd., 1978)

Waller, Jane and Michael Vaughan-Rees *Women in Wartime: The Role of Women's Magazines, 1939–1945* (Macdonald Optima, 1987)

Books for older readers

Braybon, Gail and Penny Summerfield *Out of the Cage: Women's Experiences in Two World Wars* (Pandora, 1987)

Cunningham, Valentine "Women Writing Spain" in *Spanish Front, Writers on the Civil War* (OUP Paperbacks, 1986)

Enloe, Cynthia *Does Khaki Become You? The Militarization of Women's Lives* (Pandora, 1983)

Kamester, Margaret and Jo Vellacott, eds. *Militarism Versus Feminism, Writings on Women and War – Mary Sargant Florence, Catherine Marshall, C.K. Ogden* (Virago, 1987)

MacCurtain, Margaret "Women, the Vote and Revolution" in *Women in Irish Society, The Historical Dimension* (The Women's Press, Dublin, 1978)

Macdonald, Sharon and Pat Holden and Shirley Ardener, eds. *Images of Women in Peace and War, Cross-Cultural and Historical Perspectives* (Macmillan, 1987)

Ridd, Rosemary and Helen Callaway, eds. *Caught up in Conflict, Women's Responses to Political Strife* (Macmillan, 1986)

Rowbotham, Sheila *Hidden from History* (Pluto, 1973)

Rowbotham, Sheila *Women, Resistance and Revolution* (Allen Lane, 1972)

Schreiner, Olive *Woman and War*, 1911 in *An Olive Schreiner Reader* ed. Carol Barash (Pandora, 1987)

Terry, Roy *Women in Khaki, The story of the British woman soldier* (Columbus Books, 1988)

Van Voris, J. *Constance de Markievicz, in the Cause of Ireland* (University of Massachussetts Press, 1967)

Wiltsher, Anne *Most Dangerous Women, Feminist Peace Campaigners of the Great War* (Pandora, 1985)

Glossary

Allies Those nations allied by treaty against Germany and the other Central Powers in the First World War; in the Second World War, those nations allied against Germany, Japan and their backers. In both wars, Britain was one of the Allied nations.

anti-semitism Prejudice or discrimination against Jews.

auxiliary Helping, giving support.

censor To ban, or cut something out of, a publication that is thought to be in some way harmful or dangerous.

civilian A person not in the armed forces.

combat A fight or a battle.

combatant A person who takes part in fighting.

communist A person who believes in communism – the political and economic theory that advocates a classless society in which private property has been abolished and the means of production belong to the community.

concentration camp A place in which prisoners of war are kept under guard. Many of the Nazi concentration camps in the Second World War were also death camps.

conscientious objector A person who objects to war and refuses to fight because she or he believes that it is wrong to kill.

conscription A system of making people join the armed forces.

demobilize ('demob') To release troops from military service, usually because of a return to peace after war.

deterrence The theory that possessing nuclear weapons will stop (or deter) an enemy from attacking your nation because of the threat of retaliation.

dilution The practice of dividing up the work of a skilled man among several unskilled women.

emancipate To set free from political or social restraint and oppression.

empire A group of countries under one ruler.

evacuation The movement of people out of an area; for example, the removal of city children to the countryside or abroad in the Second World War.

famine A severe shortage of food.

fascism An extremely right wing political system, which historically has not respected democratic institutions and has gone to any lengths to take power. **Fascists** are typically racist and nationalist.

feminist An advocate of women's rights, who believes that men and women are equal.

franchise The right to vote in elections.

Front, the In a war, the place where the fighting is going on.

gender Classification according to sex – as masculine or feminine.

genocide The deliberate extermination of a people or a nation.

heir The person who will inherit someone's title or possessions. The **heir** to a throne becomes king or queen.

imperialism The policy of forming an empire or extending a nation's influence and power by getting control over other nations.

intern To put someone in a prison camp.

liberation Freedom from oppression or enemy occupation.

militant Ready to fight.

militarize To equip and make ready for war.

military About soldiers or the armed forces.

missile A weapon that is sent to its target in a rocket. Nuclear missiles can be sent in a rocket.

munitions Military supplies, especially weapons and ammunition.

nationalism The desire for, or policy of, national independence.

nationalist An enthusiastic supporter of her or his own nation, who considers national interests more important than international interests.

Nazi A member of the German National Socialist Party, the fascist political party that controlled Germany under Hitler's leadership in the Second World War.

nuclear To do with atomic energy, which is released when the nuclei of atoms are split or combined together.

occupation In war, the taking over of another country by armed forces.

pacifist A person who believes that war is wrong.

patriotism Devotion to one's country and willingness to defend it.

rations In war, the official allowances of each person for food, clothing, and other goods.

republic A State in which the power is held by the people or by the people's elected representatives.

republican A person who supports a **republic**.

Resistance, the In the Second World War, the underground organization in France that fought against the German occupying forces.

siege In war, the surrounding of a town or city and attacking it from all sides.

skilled Trained and experienced.

suffrage The right to vote in elections.

suffragette A woman who used **militant** tactics in the British struggle to win the vote for women.

suffragist A woman who agitated for the vote in Britain but did not agree with the use of **militant** tactics.

trenches Long, narrow channels cut in the ground, used in war to cover and conceal troops in battle.

volunteer A person who offers to do something of her own free will and sometimes without pay.

warhead The explosive head of a **missile**.

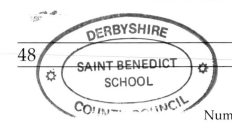

Index

Numbers in **bold** indicate illustrations.